MY DAD SURVIVED 9/11!

US History for Kids Grade 5

Children's American History of 2000s

Speedy Publishing LLC

40 E. Main St. #1156

Newark, DE 19711

www.speedypublishing.com

Copyright 2017

People say, "On 9/11, everything changed." Let's look at the terrible attack on the United States that day, and the stories of two people who survived it.

SET THE SCENE

A small body of people, with a lot of resources and a lot of hate, have been working for decades to changes governments in the Middle East. They are Muslims, but very few people who follow Islam believe or act as these people do.

MUSLIMS IN A MOSQUE

WESTERN PEOPLE MARCHING

People in western countries hear about these angry, violent groups when they make attacks in Europe or North America, but most of their attacks have been against other Muslims, in Muslim countries.

Osama bin Laden, from Saudi Arabia, founded one of these groups, al Qaeda. Al Qaeda wants to establish a pure Islamic state in the Middle East, with their idea of "pure" being a very traditional, minority view of what Islam teaches. To reach this goal they want to reduce the influence of the United States in the Middle East, to destroy the state of Israel and force all Jews to leave the area or die, and to change the way all the Arab states in the Middle East are governed.

OSAMA BIN LADEN

AL QAEDA FLAG

Groups like al Qaeda have only convinced a tiny fraction of the Arab world to follow them. So they regularly resort to violence to make people afraid and to disrupt nations.

A HATEFUL ATTACK

Bin Laden developed several plans for attacking the United States. He knew al Qaeda could not defeat the United States in any sort of open fight, so his plans involved kidnappings, bombings, and sneak attacks.

Over time he developed a plan to cause massive damage in the United States, to disrupt the country, and to cause the most amount of fear and anxiety. He sent almost twenty members of al Qaeda into the United States.

WORLD TRADE CENTER AFTER ATTACKS

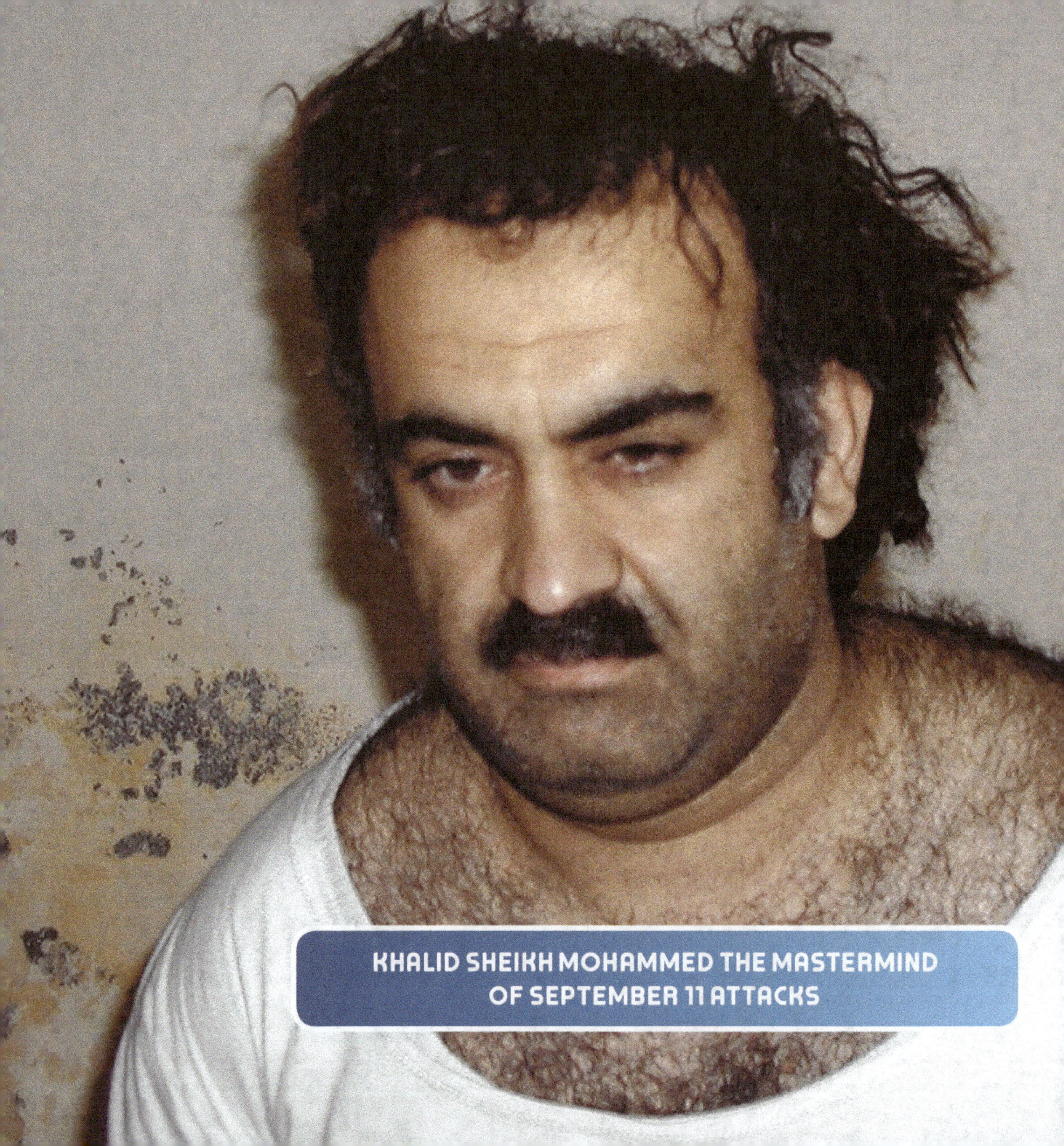
KHALID SHEIKH MOHAMMED THE MASTERMIND
OF SEPTEMBER 11 ATTACKS

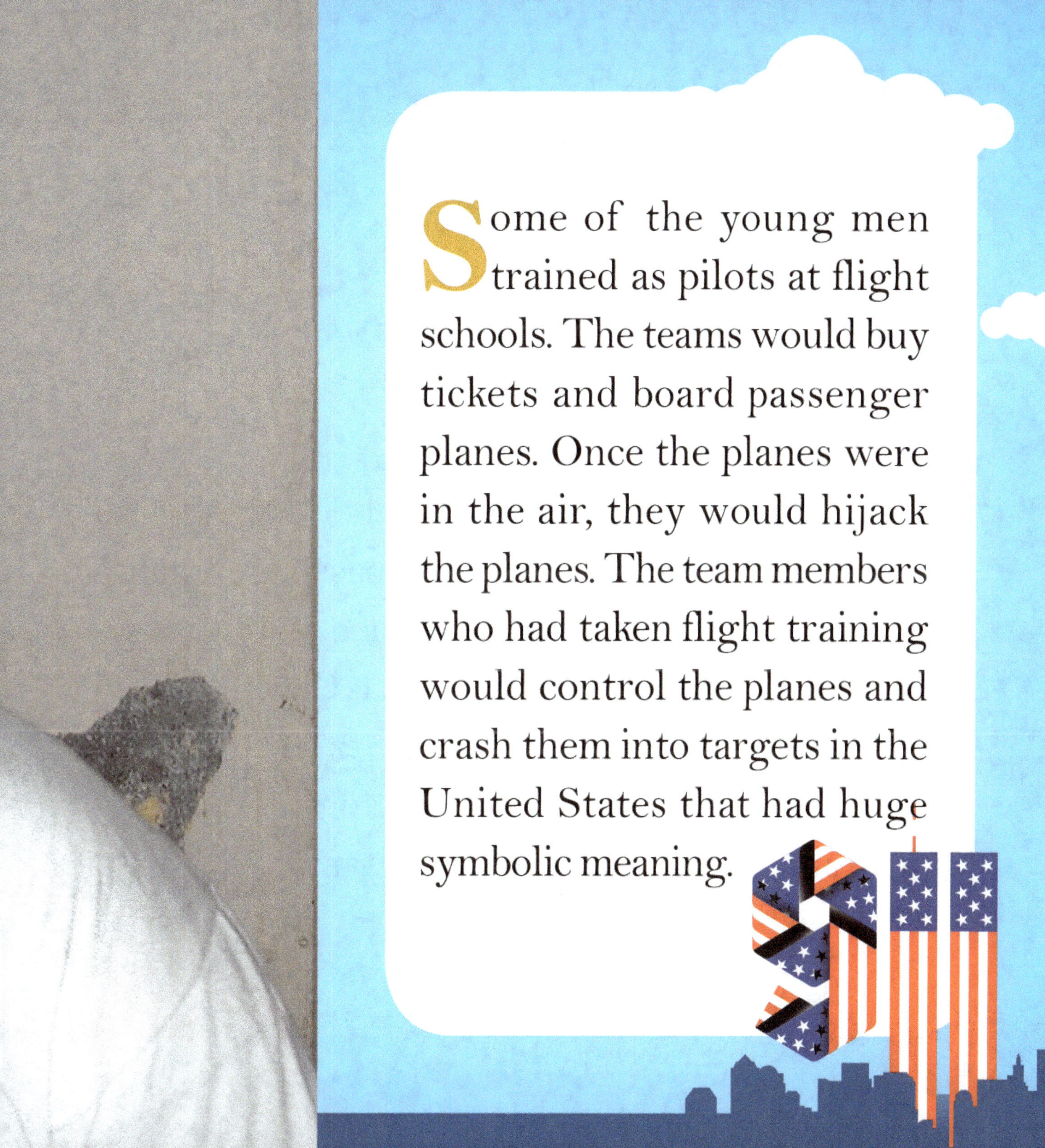

Some of the young men trained as pilots at flight schools. The teams would buy tickets and board passenger planes. Once the planes were in the air, they would hijack the planes. The team members who had taken flight training would control the planes and crash them into targets in the United States that had huge symbolic meaning.

DEATH AND DESTRUCTION

On the morning of September 11, 2001, al Qaeda teams hijacked four passenger planes during their flights. They crashed two into the World Trade Center in New York City, a symbol of the power of the United States financial system. Another plane crashed into the Pentagon, the headquarters of the U.S. military.

9/11 WORLD TRADE CENTER ATTACK

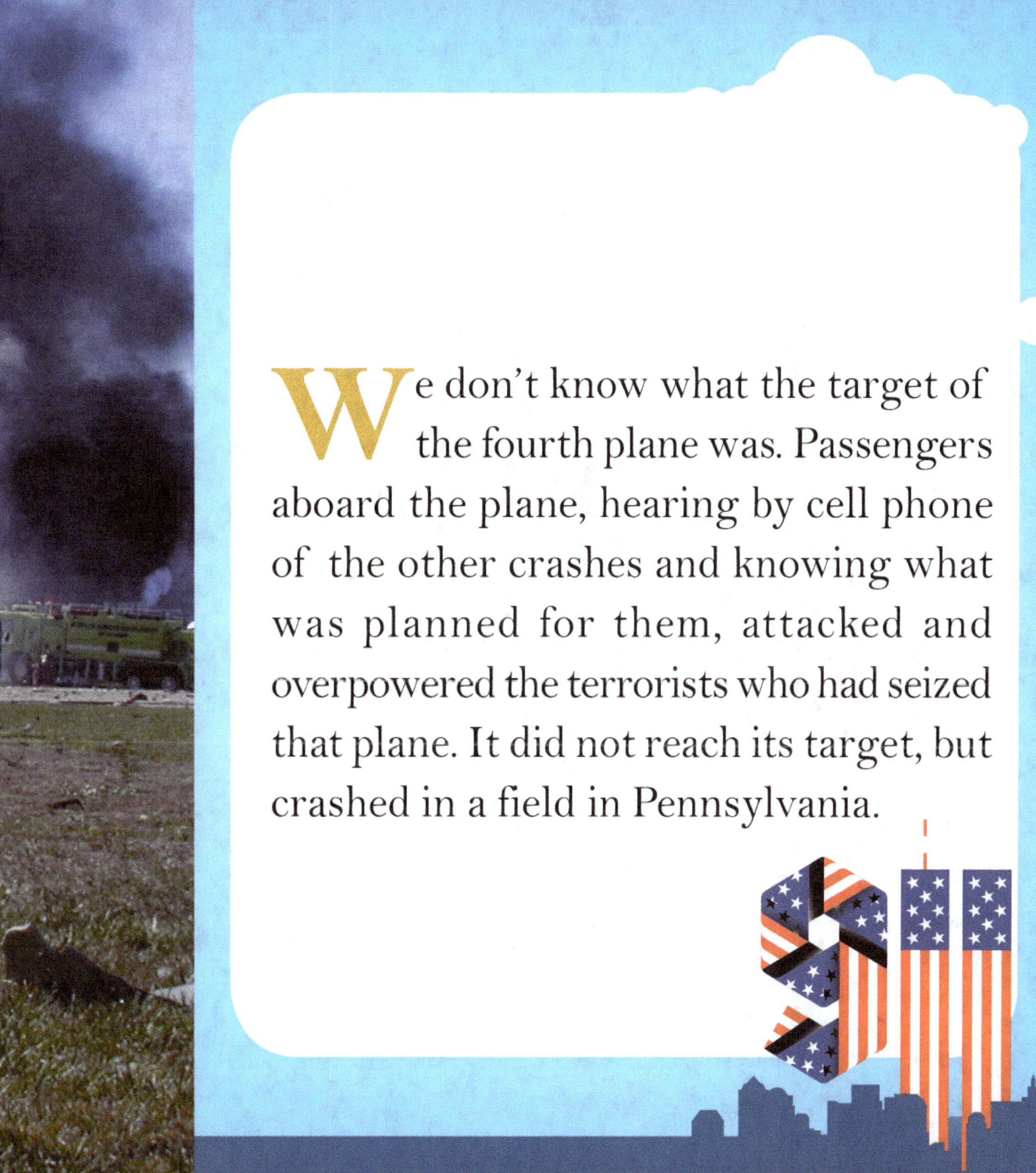

We don't know what the target of the fourth plane was. Passengers aboard the plane, hearing by cell phone of the other crashes and knowing what was planned for them, attacked and overpowered the terrorists who had seized that plane. It did not reach its target, but crashed in a field in Pennsylvania.

THE PENTAGON WAS DAMAGED BY
FIRE AND PARTLY COLLAPSED.

In the crashes, the 265 people who were on the planes all died. In and around the World Trade Center, more than 2,600 people died. At the Pentagon, another 125 people died.
More than 90 countries lost citizens.

SURVIVORS!

As horrific as this sounds, it could have been far worse, even leaving aside what the target of the fourth plane might have been. There were over 14,000 people in the two main buildings of the World Trade Center when the planes hit, and the great majority were able to find their way to safety.

Most of those who survived were in offices below the floors where the planes crashed; the people who were above those floors had no way to get out of the buildings.

DUST COVERED 9-11 VICTIMS

Here are the stories of two survivors.

JANICE BROOKS

Janice Brooks worked in the South Tower at the World Trade Center, on the 84th floor. When the first plane hit the North Tower, she and her colleagues heard a mysterious boom but did not know what was going on. Her manager told them all to leave as fast as they could. As Janice and her colleagues went to a staircase and started the long walk down to the ground, they could feel heat from the immense fire caused by the jet fuel burning in the other building.

They went down many floors. Then there was a loud-speaker announcement that everybody should return to their offices, so they started climbing back up the stairs. She fell behind the four other people from her office that she had been walking with. They made it back to their office and were there when the second plane hit the South Tower. Janice was still several floors below, and survived. Her four co-workers died.

WORLD TRADE CENTER COLLAPSED

Janice and the people around her were alive, but some were horribly wounded. They tried to start down the stairs again, but the stairs were not there any more.

They had to find their way through smoke and debris to another exit door. They had the great good luck to find the last surviving staircase in the building.

The group of survivors started down the stairs in a confusion of smoke, water from burst pipes, broken glass, and wounded people. Janice was injured and could barely walk, and finally another co-worker picked her up and carried her the last few floors to ground level, and out into the World Trade Center Plaza.

NORTH TOWER AND 6 WORLD TRADE
CENTER BEFORE 9-11 ATTACK

WORLD TRADE CENTER PLAZA AFTER THE ATTACK

The plaza was covered with broken glass, fragments of the building, fragments of the plane...and human bodies. It was only at this point that Janice began to understand how large a disaster she had just survived.

Firefighters and police officers were trying to keep order and get people to safety. They told Janice and the others to run away from the World Trade Center without looking up. They made it out of the plaza before either tower fell down.

DEPUTY
CHIEF
F.D.N.Y.

FRED EICHLER

Fred Eichler was in a meeting room in his company offices high in the North Tower of the World Trade Center. He and others actually saw the first of the two planes flying toward them. The plane seemed to be flying right at the height of their floor. They could see the company markings on the plane,but nobody in the room believed the plane would actually hit the building.

At the very last moment the plane pulled up and to the right. It hit the building around floor 94, eleven floors above where Eichler was standing.

The plane was carrying over 10,000 gallons of fuel, which caught fire immediately. Everyone in Eichler's office was tumbled to the floor, knocked over by a shock wave from the crash. The building quickly filled with smoke.

ichler called 911 and reported they were trapped. Soon a firefighter appeared and led them to an emergency exit. This staircase would take them down a few floors, and then they would have to go to a different staircase.

HELP!
EMERGENCY
NUMBER
911

Eichler did not know the firefighter's name. He went back to help other survivors, and did not survive the collapse of the tower.

The people from Eichler's office went down the stairs as directed, using flashlights to find their way. Firefighters coming up passed them and assured them the stairs were clear down to the ground.

When they were around the 20th floor there was a huge explosion and shock wave. The air filled with smoke and soot. That was the South Tower collapsing.

When they got to the fifth floor, they found the way ahead too filled with smoke and debris. Firefighters told them to go as quickly as they could to another staircase.

TOWER COLLAPSING

WORLD TRADE CENTER WRECKAGE

Pieces of the building were falling around them, including a whole elevator shaft that collapsed out of its wall and crashed to the ground.

At the ground floor, Eichler had to crawl through a broken window to get out of the North Tower. He called his wife to tell her he was all right, and she interrupted him to tell him to run as fast as he could. Then the firefighters started shouting for people to run, and Eichler and the other survivors ran.

They made it to safety about four minutes before the North Tower collapsed, about an hour and a half after the plane had hit the building.

RESCUE WORKERS RAN INTO DANGER

As people were trying to get out of the World Trade Center, brave firefighters, police officers, and doctors were trying to get in. They wanted to help as many people as possible get to safety. They knew people were trapped behind doors that had jammed, or lost in the smoke, or threatened by fire. They went into danger to help others, without thinking about themselves.

Over four hundred firefighters and other emergency workers died as the World Trade Center towers collapsed.

GROUND ZERO

OSAMA BIN LADEN

LIFE IS FRAGILE

It does not take a monster like Osama bin Laden to make our life uncertain. An accident or an illness can change everything, so we are no longer able to do what we hoped to do.

Uncertainty is part of life. The only parts we can be sure of are the past, that we have already lived through, and what we are doing right now.

We should try to make our every moment as useful, as interesting, and as joyful as we can.

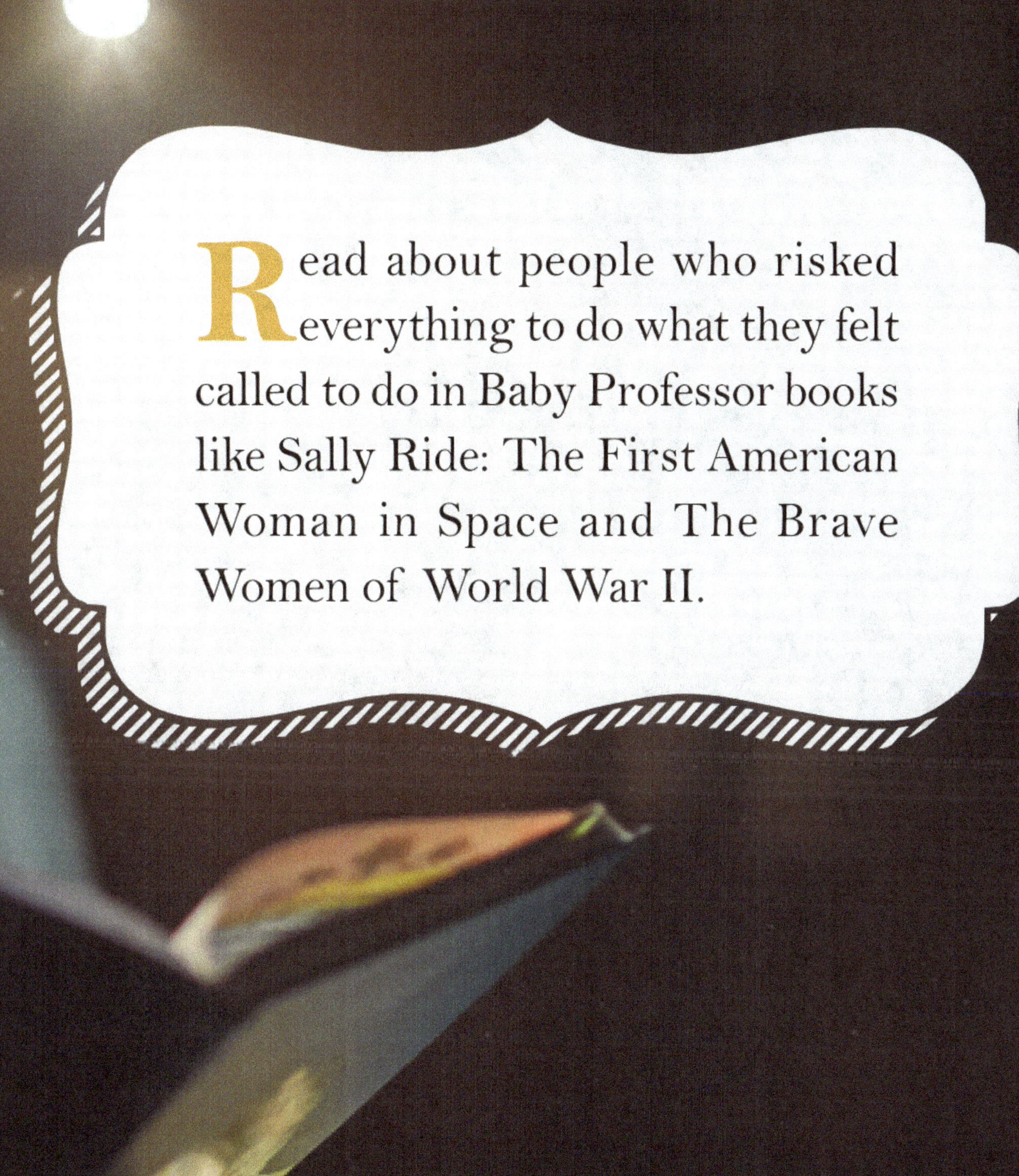
Read about people who risked everything to do what they felt called to do in Baby Professor books like Sally Ride: The First American Woman in Space and The Brave Women of World War II.

Visit

BABY PROFESSOR
EDUCATION KIDS

www.BabyProfessorBooks.com

to download Free Baby Professor eBooks
and view our catalog of new and exciting
Children's Books